Gaitherins

Fae

Annie's Kist

**A selection of poems and sayings
from the Buchan Area
of N.E. Scotland**

**Collected by Annie Shirer
Edited by Jim Shirer**

ISBN 1-900173-45-X

First published December 2000

By

Aberdeen & N.E. Scotland
Family History Society

Printed by:-

RAINBOW ENTERPRISES,
          Unit 2, Saxbone Development Centre, Dyce, ABERDEEN

CONTENTS

Photograph on cover.(taken about 1905 at Loch Hill Cottage, Kininmonth)

R.H. Side, Annie Shirer. 1873 – 1915

L.H. Side, Maggie Shirer.1863 – 1916

Centre, Kenneth McLean Shirer, her uncle. 1822 – 1913

Introduction

As a boy I spent my summer holidays at East Loch Hills Kininmonth, where my paternal Grandmother Elizabeth Shirer (m.s. Roger) farmed. Also there were my Uncles Davie and Wullie and Aunt Jessie Anna.

On Sunday afternoons, especially if it was wet, I was allowed through to the parlour, and there I was allowed to rake through a box called Annie's Kist. In this box were innumerable items from bygone days. Names I remember now meant nothing to me then, names like Peter Buchan, Gavin Greig, Jessie Saxby and John Stuart Blackie, places such as Shetland, Dysart, Edinburgh and even Whitehill New Deer, a mere twelve miles away were wondrous places to a young boy. This collection of poems and sayings is based on a small part of the collections of Annie Shirer, a cousin of my Grandfather James Shirer (1856 ~ 1934) and are totally separate from the massive collection of material she gave to Gavin Greig, who described her as, his KININMONTH LASSIE.

Annie was born at Atherb, in the parish of New Deer, the illegitimate daughter of William Shirer (1826 ~ 1906) who was known as Aul Cyarnie, he farmed at Cairncummer Auchnagatt, and one of his servants, Jessie Fiddes. It took me years to find her birth, as she was registered as Annie Innes Fiddes. As a baby she was taken to be brought up by my Great Grandparents Kenneth McLean Shirer (1822 ~ 1913) and Margaret Clarke (1835 ~ 1892) at Cairncummer.

Annie, and her cousin Maggie Shirer, her senior by ten years were dressmakers and my late Aunt Mary often spoke of a lot of people visiting Loch Cottage at Kininmonth where the women got fitted out. She also mentioned that Annie 'raked the countryside' collecting various songs and poetry for Gavin Greig.

Annie was also a member of the RHYMOUR CLUB in Edinburgh, a group of people interested in preserving the historical songs and literature of Scotland.
This is obviously how Annie got in touch with some of the notable authorities in this field, who not only wrote to her, but visited her at Kininmonth.
Of particular interest was her friendship with Millie, Duchess of Sutherland, another enthusiast, and daughter of the Earl of Roslyn, and in one volume of the Transactions of the Rhymour Club, we find Annie described as ' The Marchioness of Mintlaw '.
Little did they know at that time, nor did I until some eighteen months ago, that Annie had on her father's side, the Kings of Scotland and England, and also St. Margaret of Scotland.

Annie, after nursing her Aunt Maggie for some years, became ill in November 1915, and died at Aberdeen Royal Infirmary 24th December 1915, and it was by finding her death certificate I was to establish who her mother was.

Rest in peace my bonnie lass
I found yer Mither

Jim Shirer.
Rho-Mar
Elrick
2000

General Rhymes

Charlie sells the needles and preens,
And Charlie sells the trappin';
And Charlie has a pair o'blue een,
Ti' keep the lassies lauchin'.

Fortune she's a saucy jaud,
She seldom smiles on me;
She dings me here an'dings me there,
And open's my hard won fee.

Guid faith! I'm sure your pans will sell,
For brose at ilka toon;
Jist swing them on yer back my lad,
And hawk them roon' and roon'.

Yule has come, and yule has gone,
And we've a' fared weel;
Jockie's at his flail again,
And Jennie's at her wheel,
And a' the loons and lassiekies,
Are back at the skweel.

The rottans and the mice they a'fell a'strife,
And widna let my meat be until I got a wife,
When I got a wife, my wife she couldna rin,
And I got a hurl barrow, to hurl her oot and in.
The hurl barrow broke and my wife she got a fa',
Shame gang wi' the hurl barra, cripple wife an'a'.

A suppie o'kail and a drappie o'ream
They set me a-sleepin' as seen as they are deen.

The drinkin'it's a rovin trade,
And mony's the begger it has made;
And gin ye like yer wallet teem,
It's come and try the drinkin'O.

Ye needna stan'there gweedman,
Come ben and rock the cradle;
And tak'your kail and brose yersel,
Ye ken that I'm na able.

I'm but a peer misguided man,
Wi'a reekie hoose and a rinnin' oot pan,
A girnin geet and a wife to ban.

I've a sair back, and I've sair beens,
Ca'in' Mill o' Waukie's auld hoose stanes.

Ye had surely had your een tied up,
For yon's a seein' evil;
He winna work, he winna wint,
He's jist a drunken deevil.

There's naething on the horsie but the hair and the hide,
The gut and the gaw;
Little horsie brak's back and baby gets a fa'
(said by a mother when dandling a child on her knee)

Gang and tell yer Auntie Bell,
To buy a bottle o'soor ale;
The morn is the market day,
And ye'll hae nae mair ti say.
(said in scorn to a tale bearer)

He's jist as fat as a butter ba',
I doot their kirn disna offen ca'.
(said of a fat lazy person)

A little health,a little wealth
A little house wi'freedom;
And at the end a little friend
And little cause to need him.

Fill a pot, fill a pan, fill a blind man's han;
Them that has and winna gie,
Crooket will their bairns be.

I widna hae a baker ava,'va 'va,
I widna hae a baker ava,'va 'va
For he sits and he cracks
And he burns a his babs
And I widna ha'e a baker ava,'va 'va.

Ye'll hae me doon tae Peterheid,
Bit dinna leave me there;
Ye'll bring me back to Crimond,
Wi' muckle glee and care.
Show me at the Wilsons Wells,
But dinna leave me there,
But ye'll bring me tae Cairnie's toon,
And ye'll gie me tae Jockie Thom,
That drives second pair.
(postal directions on a 1842 Valentine)

D'ye ken the wye tae try a freen',
Gin ye hae een ava;
Instead o'gi'en ae pound note,
Jist seek the len o'twa.

They sudna hae a horse
That canna hau'nle the whip;
And they sudna ha'e a man,
That canna hand him up.

When the mist is on the sea,
Scarce o' water we will be;
But when the mist is on the hill,
We'll get water tae oor mill.

Did ye see the gill stoup, the gill stoup, the gill stoup,
Did ye see the gill stoup half fu'o'ale?
I saw the gill stoup, the gill stoup, the gill stoup,
But fit's ahin the gill stoup, I winna tell.

My hert's in the Heilins,
My claes is in the pawn;
And my wife's awa' to Paisley
Wi' another wife's man.

Counting Rhymes and Games

Frae Wibleton to Wableton it's sixteen miles,
And frae Wableton to Wibleton it's sixteen miles,
Back again and fore again, it's thirty two miles,
This wey and that wey, and baith weys whiles.

A'body's bonnie to somebody's e'e,
Rich man puir man, tink man tee.

Eerie, Ane, aickerty Ann,
Quiver, quaver, Irishman;
Feelsam, falsam, mixim Jock,
Stinklim, stanklim Buck!

A.B.C one, two, three,
Dinna coont the bonnie lass,
For oot goes she.

An tan toose Joe,
Up the hill and doon ye go;
First a shoe, and syne a boot,
I choose you oot.

I met a wee bit maiden wi'a wee bit man,
She carried in her wee bit han, a wee tin can;
The wee bit man wad kiss'er and the wee maiden ran,
And oot o' her wee handie fell the wee tin can.

One, two, three, four, five, six, seven,
Eight, nine, ten, and oot goes eleven.

Inkie, pinkie, tirlie, winkie,
Sat upon a steen binkie;
Steen binkie doon did fa',
Wi'inkie, pinkie neist the wa.

4

Sing a song a ming a mong,
A carlin and a kit;
And them 'at disna like butter,
Put in their tongue and lick.

Owre Don, owre Dee, Owre the lea cam ye tae me,
Owre the lea cam ye tae me, skip the rigs o' BALLACHREE;
Ballachree and Jockie Snipe, steal't the tail fae ma tyke;
Frae ma tyke, and frae ma ram, kent ye blind Tam?

Tak'up yer fit and gie's a pu',
Sax wiks hae I been fu';
Sax mair I shall be,
By the land and by the sea;
A' the tailors in the toon,
Up the bank and syne doon.

Said the haddock to the skate,
Skip the creel, and shun the bait;
Said the herrin' to the eel,
Crook your little tail weel;
Dear bocht, dear sauld,
Seek a sheep fae Jock's fauld;
Jock's fauld's very close,
Tak' the tail fae Jock's horse.

There was a miller stout and bold,
Fed upon beef and brose;
He's sturdy legs and shoulders broad,
As ye may well suppose.

Hop, hop, hop, we're off to the shop,
To buy some nice new toys;
And Jock will come and buy a drum,
For he likes to mak' a noise.

5

Mister Mundy, how's your wife?
Very sick and like to die;
Has she got any butcher meat?
Yes, as much as she can buy;
Half a horse, half a coo,
Three quarters o'a soo;
She mak' her porridge afa thin,
A pun o' butter she pits in;
Whyles a fish, and whyles a fin,
You're oot and I'm in!

I am a little maiden, free from sin or strife,
But when I'm big I will be a very happy wife;
And so will you all, except one, two, three,
And she'll die a maiden, and oot goes she.

Where are you going, little Sally Brown?
Up to the garden, an apple to bring down;
I'll give it to the best girl here that I see,
But not to this pretty girl, and out goes she.

Hush ba, baby, dinna mak' a din,
And ye'll get a fishie, fin the boat comes in.

There's a neat little clock, in the centre it stands,
And it points oot the 'oors wi' it's twa pretty hands;
The een shows the meenits, the ither the 'oors,
As aft as ye look to yon high church toors.

Me and my Grannie, and a great lot mair,
Kicket up a row gaun hame fae the fair;
By cam the watchman and cried , Wha's there?
Me and my Grannie, and a great lot mair.

We'll wash oor face, and kaim oor hair,
And oot to sniff the caller air;
Syne aff for fairin' to the fair,
At sax o' clock in the mornin'.

6

Rhymes of General and Local Interest

A Deft Refusal

If fae yer glove ye tak' the letter G,
Your glove is love, and that I offer thee.
This was sent to a young lady by her admirer a Mr Page
She replied:-
If fae yer Page , ye tak' the letter P,
Your Page is age, and that's nae use ti' me.

The Sappy Seat

On the son of a local blacksmith who was a
Candidate for the ministry of a Buchan Kirk.

He'd lik a kirk in which to preach,
A place wi' muckle siller man;
But we'll keep him from the sappy seat,
The smith's a gallant fireman

The like of him to preach and teach,
And young dames for to session man!
We'll haul him oot pit Tamson in,
The smith's a gallant fireman.

Lovers Toasts

Here's to them that's far awa',
And in a foreign land;
And here's to him that stole my heart,
And winna tak' my hand.

Here's to them that I love best,
For fear they love nae me;
But here's to you and your sweetheart,
And mine, whar e'er she be.

Here's to you in roses red,
Here's to me in thyme,
Here's to you and your sweetheart,
And here's to me and mine.

A green path, a gravel walk;
A bonnie lass, and time to talk.

The Way to Shear

Did you ever hear o' the wye to shear?
Ride ti' yer wark on the back o' a steer,
Hame fae yer wark on the back o'a meer,
Gin ye've a' thae beasts ye've nae eese ti shear.

In Praise of Snuff

It's hae my bonnie sneeshin' mull,
It's how my bonnie sneeshin' mull;
I get baith licht and wisdom bricht,
Tappin' my horn sneeshin' mull.
The pipe it gars me hack and spit,
For oot door fouk it's only fit;
But snuff's genteel, and loved by a',
In cottar's hoose, or the lairdie's ha'.

Lovers

The meetin's a pleasure,but the pertin's a grief,
And an unconstant lover's, worse than a thief;
A thief can but rob you, tak' a that ye have,
But an unconstant lover can lay ye in yer grave.

This was 'recycled' as a pop tune in the 1950's

Crichie Wives

The auld wives o' Crichie haud a gey Aiky Fair,
They danced roond the tents wi' their jiggers a' bare.

Local Quips

Ridinghill's women are foul fisher jauds,
Causewayhill's women they lie wi' the lads;
Willie Smith's women are aye neat and clean,
But the diamonds at Lochhills wad dazzle yer een.

O, lassie are ye sleepin' yet? If no jist come and speak,
A meenit ti' yer Chairlie, and gie him some ill cheek;
I winna see ye noo sae aft as I hae deen afore;
But I'll maybe come and see ye when I gang ti' Kintore.

There's plenty o' Donside caffies
And plenty o' Donside Kye;
And plenty o' bonny lassies,
If the laddies were na sae shy.

Here's tae them that's black and tarry,
Deep in love and daurna marry;
If he were here that's far awa',
I wadna smile tae you ava.

I'll tak this gless into my hand,
And drink to a' that's here;
There's nane can tell where we may be,
Afore anither year,
Some may be wed, some may be dead,
Some may by lyin'low;
Some may be on a foreign shore
and ken nae where to go.

Advice to Maids

Maidens fair tak' my advice,
As lang's yer young and bloomin',O;
And never spend your idle time,
Wi' young men in the gloamin',O.

Sailors they are bonnie chappies, O,
But they are neat and clean;
They can kiss a bonnie lassie,
In the dark and no' be seen.

At the big toon o' Potterton,
There's neither watch nor clock,
But it's "Porridge Time" or " Sowen Time",
Or else "Yoke! Yoke!"

9

In Derision of Masters

Awa wi' yer tatties, yer sowens and yer kail,
Yer ill- baken breid and yer sour brown ale;
Wi' cauld kail and tatties, ye feed us like a pig,
While ye drink tea and toddy, and hurl in a gig!

A Lilt of Old Age

Aince I hid a feather bed,
Wi' curtains a' aroon',
Bit noo I have to lie upon,
A Cauff shakkie doon.

The Darger

Up to the knees amon' dubs and clay,
Up to the knees amin water;
Altho' I'm only a darger chiel,
I'll mairry my maister's daughter.

A toast: On a Dismissed Servant.

Here's to him that's turned oot,
But nae to him that turned him oot;
May the deil turn him inside oot,
That turned a fellow craiter oot.

A toast: On the New Year

The auld year has gone, and the New Year has come,
Wi' pleasures to plenty, and sorrows to come;
But I'll tak' up my gless, and I'll drink it wi' cheer,
For a health to you a', and a Happy New Year.

A Buchan Valentine

" As sure's a gun 'twas a for fun,
That I did lichtlie you,
Forget, forgie's puir witless me,
For this will never do.
Come back, come back to Birlnyak,
On Friday nicht at nine;
Let bygones be bygones wi' me,
And be my Valentine!"

A Cure for Love

Oh! dear, Doctor! What'll cure love?
Nothing, said the Doctor that I know of,
Then said the lady, I must die!
Well, said the Doctor , what care I?

Fishermans Toast

Here's to the keel, and here's to the skate,
I canna get as muckle, as mak' a diet o' meat.

To a Snail

Snailie, snailie set oot yer horn,
And I'll gie ye milk and breid the morn.

Rin and catch the mail coach,
Rin and catch the mail;
Four and twenty gentlemen
Chasin' at a snail.

In the year 1830, a John Henderson was tried for smuggling, at the JP Court of Old Deer. He brought himself off by the following special pleading in rhyme:-

Here's John Henderson dwells in the moss o' Savock,
He's nae breid in his hoose, nor meal in his pock;
His bairns are a' barfit, and his wife wints sheen,
And gin ye fine him, gentlemen, ye'll never be forgien.

When the aforesaid John Henderson's only cow died, he sang the following rhyme to Annie Shirer's Grandfather James Shirer (1780-1855) who was farmer at Cairncummer, Auchnagatt.

Happy the man who has no beast, nor hoose to put it in;
For he can freely tak' a rest, and naething trouble him.

Farm and Place Rhymes

It's ye'll shear the fur' lass,
And I'll shear the riggin';
And when ye come to ca'a ruck,
It's I'll dae the biggin'.

The tatties they ha'e a gane wrang,
And vexed the farmers sairly;
And gin ye chance to buy a peck,
It's man, they'll scrimp ye fairly.

Cairncake an' Cairneywhing,
Bracklemoor an'Balnamoon;
Scour the bowers of Ladysford,
And sweep the lums of Glasslaw.

Auchentumb an' Auchenten,
Auchnavaird and back again;
Auchnagorth and Auchnacant,
To see them a's a simmer jaunt.

We like a sho'er in sweet April,
When the corn is a-shawin';
And anither aboot the Lammas time,
When the barley is a-fullin'.

The term time will soon be here,
And we will a' win free;
And to yon toun I'll nae mair gang,
Gin ye wad mairry me.

When the breakers roar at Rattray Heid,
We ken the weather will be gweed;
But when they roar at Auchentumb,
A' the ill weather is to come.

He's a hareim tearem, hielin' scareim,
Roch and richt, Keen and bricht,
Common country deevil.

When ye plant the tatties, gie them three to the fit
Ane to the corbie, and ane to the man;
Wi' the third bonnie tattie to rot in the lan'.

Auld Deer, New Deer, Strichen and the Broch,
Syne we'll hae a straucht road,
And that will gar me hough (walk)

Derogatory Rhymes

Robbie Stobbie, doon the glen,
Ate his mither's aul black hen,
Be she roas'in, be she raw,
Robbie Stobbie ate her a'.

You dear, you doo, you dirty soo,
Ye needna' think that I love you;
But I send you this to let you know
How very much I am 'bove you.

" Dyod, ye min me on a sow,
as fat's a butter ba'".
"Na, na, a sow has foure feet,
and I hinna but twa."
" weel, ye're the likest till a sow
that I ever saw!"

Thiefie, thiefie, steal a neepie,
Steal a needle or a preen,
Steal a coo, or a be deen.

Jeanie Tamson is an ass,
For a donkey she would pass;
If you meet her on the road,
Be sure and greet her wi' a clod.

Hey, hon sulky John,
Big drone, the sod's on.

Rhyming Riddles

They took me from my mother's side,
And with a knife cut off my head;
Wi' confounded drink they did fill
And made me speak against my will;
I've made peace and I've made war,
I've shut up what was ajar;
I've made to lovers often smile,
That were from each other many a mile?
(A Quill Pen)

Doon in yon meadow there lies a lair,
Four an' twenty carpenters a' work there;
Some in blue bonnet, some in straw hat,
I'll say ye're a clever scholar if ye'll tell me that?
(A Bee's Hive)

Reddichie, roodichie, that runs on the dyke,
Haud awa' yer clockin' hen, and I carena for your tyke?
(A Worm)

If you tell me my name
I'll give you a groat;
It is, was, and will be,
And yet it is not?
(Not)

If three doves were on a tree
And I shot two, how many would there be?
(None; the third would fly away)

It's round, and round, and just a pound,
And disna weigh an ounce.
(A Sovereign)

As I geed in the fife coast, I met a Fife scholar,
I asked his name and drew off his glove,
And what was the name of that scholar?
(Andrew)

Four and twenty white kye stan'in in a raw,
Oot cam' the red bull an' lickit owre them a'?
(Teeth and Tongue)

Roast me weel and toast me weel,
But dinna burn my beens,
For fear ye see nae mair o' me,
Aboot yer auld fire stanes?
(A Haddock)

As I gaed tae my faither's feast,
I met a great mysterious beast;
Wi' ten tails and forty feet,
And aye the beast crept oot tae eat?
(Ten Oxen and a Plough)

Foure redrootrees, foure upstanders,
Twa lookie-oots, twa crookit boots,
Twa leatherin' cloots, and a waggie?
(A Cow)

I see something that ye canna see,
And it's as fite as fite can be?
(The White of an Eye)

As roon's the mune and as red as gold,
Oh! Sic bonnie; but oh! Sic old?
(The Sun)

It traivells on, it traivells o'er,
But never traivells to the door?
(A Clock)

It's as roon as the mill-wheel,
And luggit like a cot;
Ye may guess, and guess, a haill day,
And nivver guess that?
(A Tub)

A girl told her lover to visit her---
When the lint was drawn,
And the leaves were fa'in',
And the deid was happin' the living?
Ie. When the cover was off the table,
The table "leaves" down,
and the fire newly made up.

It's mou'ed like the mill door,
And luggit like the cat;
And tho' ye guess till Martinmas,
Ye winna guess that.
(The Mill Hopper)

It is in timmer, but nae in the tree,
It's in the mine, but nae in the sea;
It's in the dam, but nae in the water,
It's in the mill, but nae in the hopper.
(The Letter M)

When first the wedding knot was tied
Between my wife and me,
My age exceeded her's as far
as three times three does three; (ie. two thirds more)
but when ten years, and half ten years,
the 'gither we had been
her age cam up to mine as near
as eight does to sixteen (ie. half less).
He was 45, she was 15; and , after they had been
married for 15 years, he was 60, and she was 30.

My nose is long, my breath is strong,
My back it is broad, my belly is wood;
Just look at my sides- they're baith linned with leather
And I'm often used in a spell o'cauld weather.
(Bellows)

Riddles

What is greener than grass?
What is higher than the trees?
What is worse than woman's wish?
And what is deeper than the seas?
Love is greener than the grass,
Heaven is higher than the trees;
The Devil's worse than a woman's wish,
And hell is deeper than the seas.

As I gaed tae my father's feast.
I found a little pennerie;
It was painted oot, and painted in,
And painted owre wi' povertie;
'Twad Kill a bull, and bind a bear,
And kill twa thousand men and mair?
(Hunger)

Doon in the wid I once did grow,
But the saw did me destroy ;
Syne by the axe I came alive,
And noo I sing for joy.
(A Fiddle)

It's bigger than a louse,
It's sma'er than a moose,
Wi'mair doors and windocks in't
Than a kings hoose?
(A Thimble)

A King met a King – Where have you been?
I've been away hunting the roe:
Where is your dog – will you lend him to me?
Tell me his name and I will do so.
Call on him! Whistle on him, tell me his name?
I've told you twice, you must tell me again?
(Been)

As white's milk, and as blue's silk,
Strippit like a buck, and the mou sewed up?
(A Tick Bed)

"Roond and roond the rugged rocks
The raggit rascal ran,"
Tell me foo many R's is in that,
And ye're a clever man?
(none- no R's in that)

There lives a beast into the East,
And none it's age can tell;
'Twas at the heicht o'a' it's micht,
Before auld Adam fell;
It was with Noah in the ark,
With Adam in paradise;
It helpit Peter, on a day,
To gain his soul a prize;
It wears a ruffle roond it's neck,
That's never oot o' fashion;
His colour is like Joseph's coat,
And worn in every nation?
(A Cock)

Rhyming Proverbs and Sayings

Starve a fever,feed a cauld
And young man ye'll live till ye be auld.

Gin ye ha'e siller when on your quest,
Ye'll ken that ye're a welcome guest.

Here's my han', and weel agreet;
I'll gang wi you—a bargan be't.

Wash weel your fresh fish, and scum weel your bree,
For there's mony a foul-fitted beast in the sea.

If on your journey you would hie,
Keep the middle o' the road, and let sleepin'dogs lie.

Anither man's horse needs canny ridin'
And ither folk's gear needs a lot o guiding.

A little spark mak's a muckle wark,
And a little dog mak's a muckle bark.

Never lat on, but aye lat owre;
Twa and twa they mak fowre.

Never shak hands wi' your lover ower a burn,
Or ye'll sigh and moan, but he'll never return.

Them that weel can dae their wark,
Needna care wha see them, be't daylicht or dark.

Think weel, say weel but DAE weel is better;
Mony ane wants a wife Because he canna get her.

Whar need's be, the deevil drives;
Whar men is, women Thrives.
It's a guid mairt that hisna a bane,
And as guid a cherry that hisna a stane.

They wad need to ha'e a clean pow
That to their neebor cries- Nitty nowe.

Ye wad need to ha'e a clean cap
E'er to your neighbour ye cry – Nap

Better to say naething ava
Than speak for yersel' and ither twa.

The bonnie meen's upon her back
So mend yer sheen, and sort yer thack

Fat kitchen, licht purse, teem barn, peer horse.

Rise up rise up my bonnie loon,
And work while work ye may;
For weel ye ken this mornin's sun,
It winna bide a' day.

Workin' hard and livin' sober,
It's a better trade than bein' a robber.

Pit a cloot abeen a cloot,
And that will turn the wind aboot.

Never avenge a wrang that's deen,
Or ye'll see twa rogues, far there should be een.

Blest is the man that can bridle his tongue
Whether he's auld, or whether he's young:
The joke untell't, and the sang unsung,
Is a treat fae the man that can bridle his tongue.

Never flee as heich's the birds,
And never eat your ain words.

Gin ye meet a bonnie lassie, try her wi' a kiss;
Altho' she may look unco shy, she'll nae tak' it amiss.

Ye may gang the world ower,
Ye may roam far and wide;
But ye'll get the quaetest neuk,
Beside yer ain fireside.

If ye reach the tap o' the hill,
It winna be by their guid-will.

Many's the ship's been lost at sea,
For want o' tar and timmer;
And mony a lad has lost his lass,
For want o' stickin' tae her

Come a' ye rovin' young men,
And listen unto me;
And never lay your love
On the branches o' a tree;
The branches they will wither,
The leaves they'll a' decay,
And the beauties of a fair maid,
Too soon will fade away.

Though ye gang up in the mornin',
And nae come doon ere nicht;
Ye ken twa blacks dinna mak' a white,
And twa wrangs dinna mak' a richt.

Summer freends, when Summer ends,
Are aff and ower the lea;
Siccer freends when Summer ends,
Are still dear freends to me.

Them that's kittle's fickle
And them's that's fickle's easy coortit,
And them's that's easy coortit nae guid tae a man;
Sae mind this warnin', if ye can

The bairn's teeth that's first abeen,
Will never wear their marriage sheen.

If ye canna ate ye canna work,
If ye canna work ye canna wear,
If ye canna wear ye canna shear;
So shear, wear, work and ate,
And that's the wye tae' mak ye great.

It's a lazy loon that lies at rest,
And sees his neebors sair opprest,
Providin' meat for man and beast,
As they go to the shearin'.

It's nae a' gowd that glitters,
Nor yet a' siller that shines;
And a's nae ready for heaven
That gangs ti the kirk for their lines

Never try foul means when fair will do;
Never gang to law, for tho' you win, ye'll nae.

They're early up that nivver lies doon,
And disna ken the sun fae the moon.

MIXTER MAXTER

On a misadventure

What will my Grannie say when she comes hame the morn?
The broon coo's broken oot, and eaten a' the corn!

A lullaby

Cuddle in your bonnie baa, and get a bonnie sleepie,O;
And I'se awa and milk the coo, and gie to her a neepie,O.

Contentment

Gi'es my breeks and my jacket, my westcoat and my hose;
And that mak's a mannie fit for his brose.

A Toast

Here's to the kame and the brush,
Here's to the crub and the saddle;
And here's to the bonnie braw lad,
That carries the keys o' the stable.

A Threat

That's yer breid and that's yer cheese;
And I'm yer maister whenever ye please.

On a CLASH-PYOT or Tale Bearer

Clash-pyotie, clash-pyotie, sits on the tree,
Dings doon aipples,one,two, three;
One to the master, and one to the man
And one to the laddie that ca's the caravan,
But nane tae the clash-pyot; what will we gie,
Gie to the clash-pyot that sits in the tree;
A barrowfu' o' muck, and a barrowfu' o' hay,
And we will carry the clash-pyotie down to the Bay!

In derision of the name Charlie

Charlie Chat he milk'd the cat, and Dorothy made the cheese;
And feathery breeks sat at the door, and ca'ed awa the flees.

Love and Matrimony

There's true love, and fause love,
And love that loveth praise;
There's slightin love and tender love,
And love that ne'er decays;
There's meltin love and burning love,
And sweeter love than honey;
But I like best to hear o' love,
That ends in matrimony.

The Old Maids Lament

I think it is an awfu' thing – It wad provoke a saunt
That servant lassie's a'get lads, and the gentry they maun want,

On Fashion

My wife she bocht a bonnie hat, O "Dolly Vardon" style;
But it was oot a fashion afore she gaed a mile.

A Dance Lilt

Hey the ball the sowen ball,
'Twas held at CROOKITNEUK!
The ale was gaun like water,
Eneuch tae droon a deuk.
Jenny Taylor she was there,
Wi' a mou like ony fleuk;
And fa, think ye gaed hame wi'her,
But the lad wi'the crookit cleuk?
Peggy Tamson she wis there,
Wi' lace aboot her neck;
And fa, think ye,gaed hame wi' her,
But bonnie Sooter Jeck?

Sentence for Rapid Utterance

Dyod! I got an affa fleg the tither gloaming;
A ratten ran doon the rantle tree,
Het fit ower the pan helter skelter throo the fleer,
Up the trap an' oot at the garret windock;
And if it hidna been holed an strappit wi strae,
It widna hae won that gaet at onyrate.

The Auld Wife

There was an auld wife that lived in a shoe,
She had first twins, syne twins and thrice twins too;
She whippit them all soundly, and sent them to bed,
And when she went in , she found them all dead,
She went to the vrichts to get a coffin made,
She thocht for the bairns, but it was hersel instead;
She gaed up the stair to ring the bell,
But slipped her fit and doon she fell,
And got the coffin to hersel, And was buried in the aise-hole.

Buchan Proverbs

Na,na; that will never dee. That dog's owre dear:
I'll keep my bawbees, and bark mysel'.

Gin ye need to beg, beg yer leen.   (alone)

A teem wime mak's the kail fine.

Gin ye dinna ca' cannie ye'll droon the miller.

Yon's a lady wad gar ye swing the broom.

He wad rake hell for a farden   (on a greedy person)

Kick yer heels in the air and lat byganes sleep.

Ye sud ca' canny; ye've bairns o' yer ain, and ye dinna ken
wha's door may drap in the howe o' their neck.

He hasna muckle; for he's aye staunin' in the he'rt o' his wardrobe.

Ye can dee as ye like; for ye aye haud the heft and the blade in yer ain hand.

He's jist a stupid styte.   (styte, stot)

Mony ane's lum reeks wi' his neibor's coal.

He's firen' on like a five-'ear aul'.

The drink's a' drunk and the sowens a' made,
An' we'll awa hame to oor ain het bed.

Mony ane rides braw wi' his neibor's gear,
An' mony ane lauchs to hide a tear.

There's naebody ever cured wi' a hair o' the dog that bites 'im.

Awa tae Banff and be boiled in a pot.
(This is said because a quack doctor at Banff long ago
cured a disease with hot water)

Dustin Fair o' Auld Dear,
The shortest day o' a' the year.
("St Drostan's Fair," held on 22nd December)

He's like the links o' the crook, baith himsel' and his gear-gey puir.
Or,
As puir's the links o' the crook.

There's mony a fine teen played on an auld fiddle.

Ye're wheaslin' like a birsin' cock.

If ye dinna wyte on me ye can jist gang;
It's a guid thing that ye canna tak' the road wi' ye.

Never spen' guid siller seekin' ill.

It's a lazy loon that lies at rest,
An' sees his neibor sair opprest,
Providin' meat for man and beast
As they go to the shearin'!

My lad's merriet, but I'm nae carin',
I'll gang tae Peterhead an' sell fresh herrin'!

Ye're like the beggin' wives –Nae lang atween yer greet and yer lauch.

If ye say black's fite, he'll say "faith ye're richt."   (A Sly Person)

It's crawin' in my cap yet. (An injury not forgot)

A kiss frae yon ane wad be like an egg wintin' saut.

They're fond o' veal that wad kiss a calf.

They're fond o' fairmin' that harrows wi' the cat.

They're fond o' a horse that ride on the besom.

She hisna a lease o' her mou'---she jist hist frae ear to ear.
(said of a person with a large mouth)

I was sick, but nae wi' a sicht o' you onywye.
(Is said if you are ill, and another does not call to see you)

Better tak' care o' yersel'; I've seen as true a blue grow fite afore noo.
And,
I've seen a better ship sink in the sea afore noo.

If it had come a dirl o' win', it wad hae blawn her awa.
(Is said when light clad)

Na, but I winna tak' that in han'.
As the Irishman said when told to go for a cartload of dogs;
(ie. A sort of fish offal which he was ignorant of.)
Said when told to do anything which seems impossible.
Also,
There will be twa meens in the lift
And a third in the midden afore I learn to dae that.

Ye wad be a richt body to sen' for sorrow to a sick wife.
(Is said of a lazy messenger)

I'm maybe nae the rose amang the heather,
but I'm sure you're nae drawin'-room ornament onywye.
(Said if one says you are not good-looking)

Lats hear the wye ye canna, and we'll be pleased.
(Is said to a singer that says he cannot sing)
And,
Gie's the words, and we'll get the air when we gang oot.
(If he says he does not know the tune)

Ye needna soap me, for ye winna manage the shavin'
(Said to a flatterer)

She's lookit tae the meen, and lan't in the midden.
(Said of a lady who fails to get a husband)

I've seen a better-faur'd soo lookin' oot o' a rive mony a time.

He wad like to win up, but he's gey heavy at the tail end.
(Is said when a person has more pride than cash)

If that be the first lee ye hae telt, it wad hae chokit ye.

And,

If a' stories be true, that's nae a lee.

He wad hae been better if he had hae'n on a blin' bridle.
(Means that he ought not to have told what he had seen)

I'm nae sae dull's I'm duddy dressed.
(I'm not so stupid as I appear)

He should hae been deaf and blin' yon'er.

Them that sees you in daylicht,
Winna brak' the door aboot ye at nicht.

It winna come daylicht the day I mairry yon ane.

It wad need to be dark and her heid in a poke afore I kissed her.

The back o' yer head's a treat.

Mony ane speers the wye to Aberdeen that kens.

I wis gie gled to see their heels takin' doon the road.
(Is said of unwelcome Visitors)

If ye sit ahin' him, ye'll sit gie near the tail.
(Is said of a greedy person)

He disna aye ride when he saddles.

And,

His promises are like pie-crust, maun aye be broken.

I left him wi' a face that wad hae boiled tatties.
(When you say anything to make another blush)

I could hae tied his mou' wi' a strae rape.
(Said about a sulky person)

A nod's as guid as a wink to a blin' horse.

He's a stupid stirk that disna ken his ain sta'.

Aye bode a silk gown, and ye'll maybe get a sleeve o't.

Secon'-han' stuff gangs yafa' chape.

Dyod man, the beets are auld, but the pints are guid.
The'll maybe sell weel for a' that.

31

Dyod lassie, never let a man say—"She's my auld bauchles."
(An advice)

The follies o' youth are naething to the daftness o' auld age.

Ye dinna ken naething but daylicht, and its aye in afore ye wauken
(Remarked when a person says "I dinna ken")

The corn's sair needin' grin'in fin it gangs to the mill on its ain feet.

It's a fou barn that ye canna push a sheaf in at the door o'.

Corn nae horses bit fat ye ride.

The slip o' a minute is aften the regret o' a lifetime.

Never tak' a bye-road when ye can get a high-road.

If ye dee o' a birsin' skin, I wadna like to be the driver.
(A lazy person)

Ye wad be waur gin onything ailed ye.
(A complaining person)

That loon will gar mony ane saich, washin' the dishes yet.
(Is said of a bonnie lad)

The nearer even', the mair beggars.

Moty saut's guid eneuch for hairy butter.

He wad strive wi' a stane dyke.

He sets (jibs) gaun uphill, and kicks gaun doon.

Man ye're sharp, ye wad be better o' a birse en' tae tie up ye mou'.

Dinna plague me, for I canna be fashed.
(Don't bother me)

Kail at hame's nae kitchen—say the farm servants
when told they court the kitchen-maid.

He wad need a steam crane to raise him in the mornin'.

That will gar ye sleep wintin' rockin'.
(Hard work)

Bed at 9 and rise at 5, and ye will live to 95.

Never tether a caufie wintin' a sweil (Swivel)

Ca' canny if ye canna sole yer ain shoon.

Ye've seerly been taen thro' an English sharn midden.
(Is said to a person who tries to speak fine English)

Them that washes on Monday gets a' week tae dry,
Them that washes on Tuesday is nae far by;
Them that washes on Wednesday they wash wi' muckle speed;
Them that washes on Feersday aften wash for greed;
Them that washes on Friday they surely wash for need,
And them that washes on Saturday are dirty folk indeed.

It's a foul deuk that aye puddles in ae hole.

Ye'll never tear a hole in the new goon that yon ane promised ye.

Gin ye look the ither road she sits into the breetchin'.
(Is said about a lazy servant)

He wad buy and sell ye a' twice owre, and you'd never ken.
(Is said about a sly person)

It's easy learnin' the cat the road to the ream pig.

Ca' cannie, man, and she'll come tee wi' clappin'.

She's been a skep for a lang time, but the bees has never come her gait.

It is coontet very unlucky to pairt wi' a frein' near runnin' water.
.......To see the new meen owre the left shoulder,
or through glass, the first time.
To wash the bakin' bassie (basin)

And also,

To see the bottom o' your meal girnal foretells want. Hence, yon anes 'ill tak care that
Nane sets e'e nor weet on their girnal or bassie.
Meaning that they are thrifty or near-handed.

If a cock crows at midnight,
Or,
A strange dog bark at your door---Foretells a death.

To wag the crook means that ye'll lose yer hame.

To let the milk boil over on the fire, puts the cows dry.

Mucks the mither o' the meal girnal.

Mony a ane begins wi' a hen and ends wi' a herrin'.

They'll sit wi' a plack that canna flit wi' a penny.

It'll neither gar ye beg nor ride.
(Is said to anyone who owes a small sum and will not pay)

Pride and grace are never seen in ae place.

His taties min's ye on Orkney butter. It'll neither ate nor grease cairts.

They're ill about a roas'en hen that fry the feathers.

He winna come weel on, he's never fun' the win' blaw.

Tak tent and men' as lang's ye've the chance.

Tak the guid o'an auld horse as lang's ye hae him.

Bervie's Bowers

A popular old ballad,from the Mintlaw Collection of Annie Shirer.

Bervie's bowers are bonnie, They're a' built roon' aboot;
Bervie's seas are mony, As they roll in and oot;
As they roll in and oot, So do they up and doon,
My love is a boy more handsomer, He's the flower o'Bervie's toon.

Cauld and frosty is the nicht, and cauld,cauld blaws the win';
Open the door to me, he said, Oh, rise and let me in.
Cauld and frosty is the nicht, And the leaves fa's frae the tree;
And if I wis in and ye wis oot,I wid open the door to thee.

Altho' the nicht wis never sae cauld,And the frost wis never sae snell,
My father locks the door at nicht, And he keeps the keys himsel'
The keys they lie aneath his heid,Until the break o' day;
Ye canna win in, young man, she said, So ye may bound on your way.

Cauld and frosty is the nicht, And cauld, cauld blaws the win'
Open the door to me, he said, Oh rise and lat me in,
Slowly, slowly she rose up, And so shyly drew by the bar;
And she's ta'en him into her airms,For fear he'd been the waur.

And aye the lassie sighed and sighed, And aye mair did she say,---
What tarries my yellow-haired laddie, That went oot by the break o' day?
That went oot by the break o'day,she said, I'm afaid he'll never return,
For he has left me in sorrow, My folly for to mourn.

All the fish that's in the sea, They may take wings and fly,
And all the birds that's in the air,May build their nest on high;
And all the leaves on rotten trees, May flourish and grow green,
Afore that I prove false to you, You're the fairest of womenkind.

If all the hills were paper white,And all the seas were ink,
And all the woods in Noroway prepared for pens to drink,
I would sit doon and write,my dear, And praise your high renown;
Ye are my love,ye shall be my wife, And the Lady o'Bervie's toon.

The following is believed to be an original work by Annie Shirer and
was published in the Daily Free Press in 1912.

I'm old, and gray and feeble,
and my eyes are waxing dim;
These hands that were so nimble
are withered stiff and slim,
I feel that I am failing,
and my race is nearly run,
For time, and toil, and care, and pain,
their destined work have done.
I've done my duty in the world,
so far as I can think,
I've entertained the public well,
with wholesome food and drink,
I tell what no one else can say,
in this I stand alone,
That I've sold whisky ever since
the Queen came on the throne.

The Queen came on the British throne
in eighteen thirty seven,
When she was only sweet eighteen,
And I not twice eleven,
And the second generation has
nearly passed away,
and many changes I have seen,
since that eventful day.
Some have tried to banish whisky,
entirely from the land,
But could not quench the appetite,
Nor stay the keen demand,
And so the traffic yet survives,
Has thriven, and has grown
And I sold whisky ever since,
the Queen came on the throne.

Yes I've been selling whisky,
for sixty years and more,
the greater portion of my life,
a life of long four score.
I've sold it to the traveller,
who weary, needed rest,
and sometimes to refresh him,
and this was reckoned best.
I've sold it to the rich and poor,
And to the young and old,
To men of all professions,
and stations manifold,
And all throughout this region,
my name, and fame are known,
For I've sold whisky ever since,
the Queen came on the throne.

I can count the years precisely,
since first I opened bar,
But many things I cannot count,
as numerous they are,
I cannot count the number,
of gills I've measured out,
Nor count the many glasses
of porter and brown stout,
I cannot tell the number
of patrons I have had,
Of the many men and women,
whose hearts I have made glad,
But they'd mount into thousands
as can easily be shown,
For I've sold whisky ever since,
the Queen came on the throne.

I cannot count the number,
of the heavy groans and sighs,
Of the scalding tears that trickled down,
from many a woman's eyes;
from the eyes of many a mother,
whose sons were led astray,
Into the paths of drunkenness,
by older men than they
I cannot count the many deeds,
of darkness I have seen,
Nor the many things unseemly,
that I have tried to screen,
For I have witnessed doings,
That made me sigh and groan,
While I've been selling whisky, since
The Queen came on the throne.

And it was never in my heart,
to cause distress or pain,
Or vice or crime, or misery,
all for the sake of gain;
But vice, and crime, and misery,
and poverty an pain,
Are fruits of this same whisky,
and follow in its strain.
They say that sixty thousand,
are buried every year,
The victims all of whisky,
of brandy, wine and beer.
And that I have helped to swell the list,
since truthfully I own,
That I sold whisky ever since,
The Queen came on the throne.

There will come a day of reckoning,
when all will be revealed,
When the doom of frail humanity,
Will be forever sealed:
When victims of this traffic,
a grim and ghastly throng,
Will be arrayed before the eyes,
of those who did them wrong;
Of those who wove the spider's web,
And lured them to their fate,
Who, then would make atonement,
but will find is to late;
And I may reap a harvest from,
the seeds that I have sown,
For I've sold whisky ever since,
the Queen came on the throne.

I cannot count the number,
Of the oaths and words profane,
That a barrel of my whisky,
May often times contain;
I cannot count the quarrels,
and the fights that may be there,
Nor the many foolish capers,
In which the drinkers share.
I've watched and listened often,
to the noisy drinking throng,
And sometimes had misgivings that
the business must be wrong,
But money soothed my conscience,
and so the years have flown,
And I've sold whisky ever since,
the Queen came on the throne.